BOTH ENDS of the Leash

SELECTING and TRAINING YOUR DOG

BOTH ENDS
of the Leash

SELECTING and

TRAINING *YOUR DOG*

—————

By KURT UNKELBACH

Illustrated by
HARIS PETIE

Prentice-Hall, Inc., Englewood Cliffs, N. J.

Third printing......September, 1969

To my young friends and their dogs

Also by Kurt Unkelbach

RUFFIAN: INTERNATIONAL CHAMPION
MURPHY
THE DOG WHO NEVER KNEW
LOVE ON A LEASH
THE WINNING OF WESTMINSTER
THE DOG IN MY LIFE

Contents

The Best of Friends

The DOG is man's best friend for a very good reason: no other animal is so similar in living habits and needs.

He shares pet popularity with the cat. But unlike the cat, the dog is not independent and prefers the company of others. That's why wild dogs run in PACKS. Pack life means family life to them.

The pet dog has inherited that craving, and the human family he joins becomes his substitute for the pack. As a PUPPY, he has the same need for mother love as a human baby, and his DAM is as concerned

about him as any mother is for her offspring. So the family behavior patterns of dogs and humans are much the same, and that is why the pet puppy fits so well into his adopted human family's way of life.

Man's best friend is extremely adaptable. He goes wherever man asks him to go: to the desert, mountain, sea and arctic, and someday to the moon.

The dog is also man's oldest animal friend. Archaeology (the science dealing with ancient times) and zoology (the science dealing with animal life) agree that their association began over forty thousand years ago. And so he became man's first helper —in the hunt, at work, and on guard.

In those prehistoric times, the wild puppy had to fend for himself at an early age. The sooner he became active, the better his chance of survival.

For the first twelve or fourteen days, or until his eyes opened, he was entirely dependent on his dam: a completely helpless, sleeping, nursing baby.

At three weeks, his mind started to operate. He was able to move about on wobbly legs, and hear and smell things. A week later, he was able to trot, and he could digest food other than his mother's milk. Still, when he wasn't eating, he was sleeping most of the time.

In his fifth and sixth weeks, his legs were sturdier and he traveled faster. His appetite increased rapidly and he started to hunt for his own food. He was thinking more, and able to recognize danger. And sometime in his seventh or eighth week—certainly by his fifty-sixth day of life—his brain was almost as big as it would ever be.

But, his brain was like an empty warehouse. Only

a few, simple thoughts were in it. There was plenty of room for the learning that would come from experience.

That's the way a wild puppy started life and it's just about the same with the pet puppy today. Of course, the DOMESTICATED pup doesn't have to hunt for his food, and most of his learning comes from proper training. That means putting the right thoughts into his empty warehouse.

He'll learn, but he'll never know as much as his master or mistress. CANINE intelligence is far less than man's. Indeed, the dog isn't the smartest animal in the world, either. Most authorities rate him in third place, right behind the elephant and ape, and ahead of the horse and the cat.

But the dog is superior to man in some ways. His senses of hearing and smell are much keener. Pound for pound, he's faster and stronger, and he recovers much more rapidly from illness or injury. His eyes are placed in his head in a way that gives him a greater field of vision (250 degrees compared to man's 140 degrees), and a third lid covers each eye in time of danger. But while he sees more than man, he doesn't see as clearly, for he's color-blind.

So that's the dog. He comes in a variety of sizes, shapes, coats and colors. In all the world, there are some 350 distinct (pure) BREEDS of dogs, and everywhere in the world there is the MONGREL.

The mongrel is a mixture of two or more breeds and he outnumbers all of the individual breeds combined. There are those who insist that the mongrel is sturdier, smarter and more loyal than any of the PUREBREDS, but such reasoning isn't based on known facts.

The mongrel pup is almost always the result of an accidental breeding—a happening between a dog and a BITCH. In most cases, his dam is known, but not his SIRE. His PEDIGREE is a mystery, yet he represents a combination of all the good points and all the bad points in his family tree. It's all a matter of inheritance, and nobody knows just what he's inherited.

Thus, as pet material, he can be quite a risk. There's no telling what size he'll become, or if he'll turn ugly, or if he's SOUND, or if he's smart or stupid. Still, despite such risks, some of the pups do mature into fine pets—and more of them should, if only because of the law of averages: over 35 million mongrel pups are born in the United States every year, more than eight times the number of purebred pups.

The mongrel pup is really unpredictable, but not the purebred. Generations of SELECTIVE BREEDING are behind the purebred pup. Man's superior intelligence has enabled him to eliminate the poor points and enhance the strong points. The purebred's pedigree is known, and what he has inherited is known, and we can be reasonably sure of what he'll be like as an ADULT. To become the best of pets, all he needs is some simple training.

And let's not forget the purebred's social advantages: only he can compete at DOG SHOWS and OBEDIENCE TRIALS. The mongrel is never eligible for those sports, and that's a pity. He and his owner will never know the fun, excitement, rewards and satisfaction the sports offer the purebred dog and his owner.

About 150 of the world's 350 breeds can be found in the United States. Of these, more than 100 are recognized by the American Kennel Club, the non-profit organization which is dedicated to the advancement of purebred dogs and functions as the governing body of the dog fancy in this country.

While there's nothing drastically wrong with any of the A.K.C. registered breeds, some do make better children's pets than others. Breeds that were developed long ago to attack or to fight, as examples, may still carry such instincts. In moments of excitement, those old instincts can pop to the surface. So those breeds aren't on this book's recommended list.

Let's consider a few that are.

II

Ten Best Breeds
for Boys and Girls

Just as with races of people, every breed has both smart dogs and dumb dogs. The smart ones make the best pets, of course, for they respond to training. And the smart one with an even, gentle TEMPERAMENT makes the best pet of all, for he doesn't run around biting strangers and bringing the police to your door.

But how can one be sure of both intelligence and temperament in a puppy? There's only one way: purchase the pup from a reliable breeder. And how does one find a reliable dealer? Check with your local veterinarian, a member of the nearest kennel club, a professional dog handler, or write to the American Kennel Club.*

When visiting the breeder, ask to see the dam of the LITTER and any other adult, blood relatives. Thanks to inherited factors, the pups should look and act like the older dogs someday. Look for an outgoing pup, and one who has had lots of human association.

Over four million purebred dogs are born every year in this country, and the supply of good pups in

*51 Madison Avenue, New York, New York 10010. Ask for list of breeders in your area, and be sure to specify your favorite breed or breeds.

all breeds is never limited. Those of lesser quality can be purchased at bargain prices from the big pet shops, the mail-order houses and the "puppy factories"—the big KENNELS where there are always hundreds of pups on hand. But there's really no such thing as a bargain pup—or a bargain automobile, refrigerator, television set or anything else. You pay for what you get.

Happily and amazingly, purebred pup prices haven't increased very much over the past forty years. The costs of raising puppies have soared, but quality pups in most breeds can still be found for a hundred dollars or so—or just about what it costs the breeder to raise the pups to eight weeks of age. The exception is the Beagle. He can usually be found for fifty dollars, and sometimes less.

Again, your best guarantee of finding the right pup at the right price is to go to a reliable breeder. He's the only one who'll guarantee the pup's good health, provide you with a pedigree and A.K.C. registration papers, certify the pup's history of preventive shots against serious diseases, and advise you as to diet. Listen well, and forget the advice of the neighbor who claims to be a dog expert because he owned a dog when he was a little boy. The world is full of dog experts whose mothers took care of their dogs.

No matter where you live—city, suburbs, or open country—don't worry about the size of your favorite breed. Your dog will adapt himself to your way of life and the square-footage of your home. All he'll ask in return is care, companionship and love.

The ideal breed for young owners is one with both size and even temperament. The small breeds tend to be excitable and more apt to nip in self-defense. They are also very busy, constantly underfoot, and easy to stumble over and damage. And, of course, they don't have the muscle for such work as hunting or pulling a sled.

The breed with size and proper temperament should also have above-average canine intelligence, for that means response to training and a talent for learning new things.

And the right breed should also be an EASY-KEEPER, and one that doesn't require too much time and trouble in the GROOMING.

Above all, it should be a safe breed, or one with friendly instincts. Loyalty is a fine quality, but a dog who bites his master's friend because he doesn't understand his master and the friend are enjoying their wrestling match—well, that's carrying loyalty too far.

Of the many breeds which may be considered as ideal for young owners, here are the ten best:

AIREDALE TERRIER

The breed is over a century old and was developed from several other Terrier breeds and the Otterhound. An English invention, he was first used to hunt small game and proved himself expert on both land and water. He demonstrated his intelligence right from the start, and has since been trained to do almost everything, from herding to sled pulling to guarding. Today he's used to hunt big game in Africa and India, and he's famous in Great Britain

as a "lady's protector" on strolls in both city and country. Of all the Terriers, he has the most even disposition. He's also the biggest one, averaging 23 inches at the WITHERS and weighing 50 pounds. Loyal and eager to please, he's ideal for the one-dog family and will tolerate abuse (ear and tail pulling) from little children. Disadvantage: Hard, WIRE-HAIRED coat requires PLUCKING to keep in trim. Up-keep: $3.50.*

BEAGLE

He dates back to the days of King Arthur and was one of the first purebreds to come to America. The authorities aren't sure of his ancestry, but all agree that he has no equal in chasing fox and hare, two talents that helped establish the breed in the United States. Today, his U.S.A. population exceeds any other single breed: about four million. That amazing total is proof enough that he's a fine pet dog as well as a hunting dog, for not all of his owners are hunters. The breed comes in two VARIETIES, standing 13 and 15 inches; the biggest seldom top 30 pounds. "Merry STERN" describes his personality, for he's a fun lover and is usually looking for action. His short, tight coat requires minimum grooming, and that's

---

* This figure represents the cost per month of feeding an adult dog. The adult needs only one meal a day, and the quantity varies with individual dogs of a given breed. It's always healthier for the dog to keep him lean rather than fat. For example, a meal for the average, adult Airedale: 3–5 cups of dry kibble and meal, moistened and mixed with ¼ can of meat or mackerel, plus tablespoon of cod-liver oil every third day. Save money by buying dry foods in 25 or 50 pound bags. Store in metal garbage can to keep dry and safe from rodents.

one reason why he's so popular with young owners. He's the one little dog who acts as if he were much bigger. Disadvantage: Loves to roam, so shouldn't be left on his own. Upkeep: $2.50.

COLLIE

This is the breed with a royal background. He is a product of Scotland, where he was

developed as a herder of sheep some two centuries ago. His ancestry remains a mystery, although we do know that he was much smaller around 1800 than he is today, and that his herding days came to an end when Queen Victoria decided that the Collie was the breed for her. The breed achieved social status overnight, and ever since, his main roles have been that of pet and show dog. But the herding instinct remains, and small farms without an Airedale usually have a Collie. Writer Albert Payson Terhune made the breed famous in this country, and television's Lassie helped keep it that way. Don't believe everything you see on television, but this is a smart dog and he's easy to train. Males average 25 inches and 70 pounds; females are a bit smaller—as in all breeds. The breed has two varieties: Rough (long coat) and SMOOTH (short coat). The Rough is far more popular than the Smooth, although it's the same dog under the coat. Disadvantage: A barker, and the sharp, piercing barks may annoy close neighbors. Upkeep: $4.00.

ENGLISH SETTER

The oldest of the three Setter breeds (Irish and Gordon are the others) goes all the way back to sixteenth-century England and is believed to have early Spaniels and Pointers as his ancestors. This was the first of the purebreds to be used on game birds, the first of the purebred gundogs to arrive in this country, and the breed's popularity in the field has never waned. Few hunting breeds have as sweet a disposition, and none can surpass this one for sheer beauty. He's about Collie size and runs a few pounds

less. The long, flat coat always carries white, with patches and flecks of blood and tan, LIVER, orange, lemon or blue. As with all other long-haired dogs, his coat becomes a gathering place for city soot and grime. This Englishman prefers the country and plenty of exercise, but he'll adjust to city life. He's affectionate and wants to be with people, wherever they are. Disadvantages: Sensitive and can't be rushed in training; likes to set his own pace. Upkeep: $4.00.

GERMAN SHORTHAIRED POINTER

This is one of the newest sporting breeds. So new, in fact, that he wasn't developed until the early years of this century. His immediate ancestors are the old German Pointer and the English

Pointer, and in their family trees are such breeds as the Spanish Pointer, English Foxhound, and Bloodhound. The German is in his name because that's where he was developed just before World War I. The breed has been in this country since the early Twenties, but didn't achieve real popularity until after World War II. Abroad, he's used on birds and small game and for trailing deer, but here he's mostly used to point and retrieve pheasant, grouse, quail and duck. He's smart, fast, has a keen scent, and does exceptionally well in Obedience—a sure sign that he can be taught to do almost anything. His short, water-repellent coat and webbed feet make him at home on water or land. The newcomer averages out at 25 inches and 70 pounds and is apt to make a big noise when strangers arrive, but the noise is all bluff. He loves children, tolerates adults, and would rather run than eat. Disadvantage: Noisy, or ready to bark at anything. Upkeep: $4.50.

GOLDEN RETRIEVER

For a long time Russia took the credit for developing this beautiful breed. But now all the facts are in hand, and we know that England deserves the credit. Breeds contributing to the Golden were the Irish Setter, Wavy-Coated Retriever, Labrador Retriever, Tweed Water Spaniel and Bloodhound. Developed to retrieve game birds from both water and land, the Golden's long, dense, water-repellent coat helps keep him reasonably dry and warm in icy waters. The biggest stand at 24 inches, weigh about 70 pounds, and all are gentle and willing by nature. He's been in this country since 1900, and girls seem

to favor him over all the other sporting breeds. They don't seem to mind the grooming that the Golden's coat requires, and rate him as one of the more beautiful canines. While he still retains his fine hunting instincts, he's seen more in the home than the field these days, and he's become a star at the dog shows. Disadvantage: That coat. Water will matt it, and burrs and seeds will hide in it. Upkeep: $4.50.

IRISH WOLFHOUND

This giant breed has lived through a great deal of world history and traces back all the way to the days of ancient Greece and Rome. Nobody knows why the Irish didn't name him Elkhound, for he was used to chase and bring down both the huge elk and the wolf and nearly rid Ireland of both. When that happened, the breed's popularity diminished and it almost became extinct. Thanks to the efforts of a single dog-lover—a Scotchman, not an Irishman—the breed was saved and revived about a hundred years ago. So, if your heart is set on owning a big dog, this is the biggest of them all. He stands about 34 inches and in proper condition should

weigh 140 pounds. Despite his size, he's a very gentle animal and makes a perfect pony for small children. He's smart, too, and city owners claim that he soon learns not to knock over tables and lamps. Ideally, he belongs in the country, for he appreciates plenty of running room. Disadvantage: Appetite. Upkeep: $15.00.

LABRADOR   RETRIEVER

Judged in terms of field performance and numbers, this is the king of the five Retriever

SCHOOL BUS STOP

breeds: Chesapeake Bay, Curly-Coated, Flat-Coated and Golden are the others. Originally from Newfoundland, the breed was developed in England during the early part of the last century and soon established itself as the flashiest of the land and water hunting-dogs. Webbed feet, an OTTER TAIL and a short, double, waterproof coat make him a fine swimmer, and he's been known to rescue people from drowning. A gentle and affectionate dog, he comes in solid black, yellow or liver colors, stands 24 inches and weighs 70 pounds. Aside from hunting and pet duties, he's used as a guide dog for the blind, sled racing and herding. Disadvantage: Always on the go, so not for the lazy. Upkeep: $4.00.

NEWFOUNDLAND

This breed and the Labrador were close cousins two centuries ago. They were both known as ship's dogs, and both arrived in England on fishing ships at about the same time. This was the bigger dog, and he still is. The English used him to haul carts and carry packs, but in these modern times he functions mostly as companion and pet. He's a good swimmer, a fair but slow retriever, and his heavy coat requires surprisingly little care. Mellow by nature, he settles easily into family life and seems to prefer the young to the old. The "Newf" stands at 28 inches and weighs just as much as the Irish Wolfhound, but he's chunkier in build. Of the several big, TIMBER breeds, the easy-going Newfoundland has always been one of the most popular. Disadvantage: As with all heavy breeds, there's always the

danger of crippling HIP DYSPLASIA. X-rays can spot it, but not before the pup is six months old. So a *reliable* breeder is very important. Upkeep: $14.00.

POODLE (STANDARD)

Of the three Poodle varieties (Standard, Miniature, Toy), the Standard is both the biggest and the oldest. While his ancestral breeds have never been established, it is known that the Standard was developed in fifteenth-century Germany as a water retrieving dog—so he's really a sporting dog at heart. He was popular in Germany, France, Russia and England long before he won favor here, and today he's rated as the most popular dog in the world. He's also one of the smartest dogs in the world and stars in all of his many roles: from circus performer in Europe to Obedience trial winner in this country. So the breed is the easiest of all to train, and comes in a big variety of colors. Stands anywhere from 15 to 28 inches, but averages out at 24 inches and 55 pounds. Disadvantage: Coat care. Requires special CLIPPING for dog shows. If not for show, coat still needs monthly trim or it grows stringy. Upkeep: $4.00.

A ten-best list of anything is bound to create a storm, and there's no denying that there are other fine breeds for young people. But this is a list of ten, not twenty. So while the storm blows, let's consider this:

Of the ten recommended breeds, only three (Poodle, Beagle and Collie) are among the ten most popular breeds in this country. Breed popularity is decided by numbers, of course, and the nearest thing to a canine poll is the annual registration record of the American Kennel Club. Thus the breed claiming the highest number of individual registrations becomes the most popular breed. For some years now, the Poodle has been in first place. The Beagle is in third place, despite the fact that there are three times as many Beagles as Poodles.

Obviously, not all of the owners of purebred dogs go to the trouble of registering them. Indeed, the great majority of owners fail to register their dogs. So the A.K.C. records cannot be considered a true barometer of breed popularity. Close, yes, but never exact.

Nonetheless, seven of the most popular breeds are missing from our ten-best list. Here they are and here's why they're missing:

German Shepherd Dog: Noted for boldness, courage, watchfulness and protective spirit. Careful breeding can keep these strong instincts under control, but there has been too much reckless breeding. The results: Too many FEAR-BITERS, too much crippling hip dysplasia. A breed for experienced adults only.

Dachshund: Neither fast nor active, this is a difficult breed for Obedience work, and the long spinal column often results in back trouble. Personalities range from the nervous to the stubborn.

Chihuahua: Cute, but too tiny to be of much value as a playmate. Like most small breeds, he has a nervous, quick temperament. Too delicate, too easy to step on, and a much better bet for people leading quiet, sheltered lives.

Pekingese: Another small breed and one of the most affectionate. He's from the Orient, where he was developed centuries ago as a lapdog, and that remains his major talent to this day. Requires excessive coat care, and doesn't like rough

and tumble. A breed for those who put a premium on beauty.

Miniature Schnauzer: Adult dog fanciers have made this the "in" breed of the past several years, but that doesn't change the fact that he's a small Terrier at heart and has a quick, nervous temperament. If Schnauzer-minded, try the even-tempered but comparatively rare Giant Schnauzer.

Cocker Spaniel: A very popular breed for over forty years now, and that's the big trouble. Once one of the best of the small dogs, he's the victim of careless breeding by too many people out to make a fast dollar. Quality, sound cockers are hard to find and command top prices.

Basset Hound: An agreeable, comical fellow, but he's not built for speed and prefers hunting over any other activity except sleeping. Not a general purpose dog, and—like many other hound breeds—leaves a strong dog-scent indoors that some people find unpleasant.

So that's why seven of the most popular breeds aren't on the ten-best list for young people. Any of the seven breeds who may at this moment be making ideal pets for children may be regarded as the exceptions that prove the general rule.

III

Early Care and Easy Training

Eight weeks after he is WHELPED, the pup doesn't need his dam anymore, and he is ready for his new home—a world of giants, strange noises, and odd smells and objects. Compared to a human baby, he's extremely active, and it's easy to overrate his capabilities. The fact is that he is still a baby and should be treated as such. He knows next to nothing, although he's ready to learn.

He doesn't know, for example, that the next three months of his life will be critical ones for him. But we know—thanks to canine research with tens of thousands of pups—that his whole basic personality will be formed during those months. Once set, the personality is his for life and can't be changed to any significant degree. So if the pup is shy or bold or vicious or good-natured at five months, he'll always be shy or bold or vicious or good-natured.

The pup's personality, even if he's from one of the right breeds, is entirely in his new owner's hands. Mistreat him during his early months, and he'll end up either a vicious dog or a coward. But treat him with consideration and he'll become a fine friend and companion. This consideration for the pup spreads out into several areas:

Homecoming: Proud as you are of your new pup, there's plenty of time ahead to introduce him to your friends. For the first few days, the less confusion and excitement, the better. The pup still needs plenty of sleeping and tires easily, but he wants companionship when he's awake, so spend as much time as possible with him.

Pet Name: His name will become the most important word in his life, so start using it right away. The more he hears it, the sooner the pup will learn it and know it is his. No matter what his official or registered name is, his pet name should be short and not more than two syllables. A short name is easier to shout. A word is just a sound to a dog, of course, so it's wise not to give him a name that sounds like any of the command words (Sit, Stay, Stand, Come, Heel, Down). Sid and Sit, Clown and Down, Jim and Come, Lucille and Heel, are examples. Use his name when petting the pup and he'll know it's his within three days.

Handling: It hurts the pup if he's picked up by his ears or tail. He feels no pain when lifted by his front legs, but this can cause real damage. The pup's bones are still soft, they're the only ones he'll ever have, and those front legs may end up bowed and resembling the ELBOWS-OUT Bulldog. Legs pulled out at the shoulders and torn muscles are other results.

There's a right way to pick up a pup: one hand under his chest, the other hand supporting his hindquarters.

Housebreaking: The pup is too young to be concerned with good manners. When he has to go he has to go, and that's that. So you must anticipate when Nature calls to him, and get him outdoors (or on paper, if he's to be paper trained) fast! So get him outdoors:

1. First thing in the morning, last thing at night.
2. Before and after meals, and after he drinks.
3. After naps and play sessions.
4. Whenever he seems to be seeking a spot.

He'll soon associate the outdoors (or the paper) with his duties, especially if he's congratulated for each success. It shouldn't take more than four days to break in a pup.

Nights can be a different story. Common sense dictates that he should not be allowed to drink after his final meal of the day. Otherwise, there are two effective methods of cutting down night accidents. Both of these take advantage of canine nature. The dog is a neat animal and, in the wild, does not foul his den. So if he's confined in a small crate during the night, he'll do his best to keep the floor space clean. This, however, won't stop him from howling if he gets to feeling lonely. So the best method is to tie him to the head of the bed, giving him enough leash room to sit, stand or lie on his own floor pillow or rug. If kept near you, he won't howl, be sure of that. If Nature calls to him during the night, he'll make enough fuss to awaken you, and then you must get him out-of-doors in a hurry.

If it takes more than a week to housebreak a pup, then the owner is someway at fault, and not the pup.

Feeding: Dogs are smarter than cats, but dogs are slower starters. A kitten can be trusted not to overeat, but not a puppy. A healthy pup will stuff himself until he can't stand, and then he'll sit and eat more. So a pup's diet must be controlled: the proper foods in the proper amounts served the right number of times each day. All during his growing period, he'll require more food per day than he will as an adult.

A fat, round puppy is cute to behold, but he always has a foolish owner. Good health and longevity are the rewards for keeping a pup on the lean side. Excess weight will hinder the development of the pup's bones and muscles, and worms can become a serious problem.

As a general rule, the puppy is fed four times daily until he's ten weeks old, then three times until he's four months, then two times until he's seven months, and one meal a day thereafter. The amounts per serving vary with his age, breed and rate of growth.

What to feed? There are two reliable sources of information: his breeder, and your veterinarian. It's true that a vast amount of literature on the subject can be found in books and on the labels of manufactured dog foods. All of it is well intentioned, and most of it is worthwhile in a general sense.

But why wonder? Why be half right? Your puppy isn't general, he's specific. It's the same with dogs as it is with people: no two of the same breed or litter are precisely alike.

Night Music: If he's left alone during the long night hours, the average pup will spend most of the time howling and whining. Threats and harsh words won't stop him, and the only sure way of avoiding his music is to let him sleep next to his owner's bed. Even at this early age, he has a strong desire for company, and now his litter brothers and sisters are missing. So he reacts as any baby does, by complaining.

If he must be left alone, then his night music can often be avoided by providing him with consistent, low volume sounds. He's reassured by the sounds in the darkness, as if they represented the presence of friends. A ticking alarm clock or radio music often serves the purpose. The clicking sounds made by the nocturnal hamster as he races on his exercise wheel are like a lullaby to the pup.

The pup who resists soothing sounds and continues

to sing is either a little stubborn or so wise for his age that he can't be fooled.

　　　　　Collar and Leash:　Sooner or later, the pup must get used to both collar and leash. This is accomplished quickly if both are used when securing him to the bed during his "night housebreaking."

Otherwise, introduce him to the collar first, but only after he knows his name and is housebroken.

Three months is young enough. A light, thin collar is best, and it doesn't have to be strong. You're just getting him used to the idea, so that later, when you're training him, he won't even remember he's wearing a collar.

But don't just plunk the collar around his neck and leave it there for all time, or until he's outgrown it. Put it on him, play with him, and then take it off. Do it several times a day, leaving the collar on for longer periods each day. In a week, he won't fight the collar. Then comes the leash.

Again, the thinner and lighter the better. The leash doesn't have to be a big, strong one. It's for a puppy, not a wild lion. A length of curtain cord or some heavy twine will do. Tie it to his collar. Let him pull it around and play with it for minutes at a time every day. Make it a game.

On the day he accepts the trailing leash as a natural thing, the time is right to start his formal training.

There's nothing difficult about the formal training of a pup. All "formal" means is that the young dog learns to respond automatically to the six basic commands. Once he has the commands down pat, he's an obedient pet and a joy to own. He'll come when you call, remain safely at your side when you walk through traffic, sit outside the store door until you've returned, and stay off the furniture. He's a true pet, not a pest. (If you already have a dog and he's beyond the pup stage, don't despair. If he's over the age of three, then it will take a little longer to train him.)

At three and four months of age, the pup is growing like a weed and he's more interested in finding fun than anything else. So if the training is play, he's all for it. The trick, then, is to keep the training at a fun level, and this is accomplished in several ways:

(1) Short, daily training sessions. A pup's attention span doesn't last very long. Four or five minutes

is sufficient for the first lessons, and in time ten-minute sessions can be held.

(2) Praise and reward. Always praise him when he does something well, and offer tidbits as rewards for real progress.

(3) Patience. Try not to become irritated when the pup doesn't learn quickly enough to please you. The training should always be enjoyable for both the pup and you. There's no law that puts a time limit on training. So on a day when you're in the wrong mood, it's best to skip the training session.

(4) Step-by-step. Take it easy and don't try to cram too much learning into the pup's mind. Stay with the first command until he has it down pat. This will take several days, or it may take a couple of weeks. He's going to learn, so don't worry.

Now for those basic commands.

But first, meet Happy. He's an Airedale Terrier pup, thirteen weeks old, and he knows what his name is. Just a few minutes ago, Happy decided that the long leash trailing from his collar wasn't going to bite him. So he's been trotting around and paying no attention to the trailing leash. He's ripe for learning "Come!"

"HAPPY——COME!"   Ideally, the training for this command should start indoors—a garage or a room where there are no distractions. The lesson begins with you and the pup at opposite ends of a ten-foot leash.

"Happy (pause), Come!" is the command. Say the words firmly, but not unpleasantly. The first word, his name, gets the pup's attention. He knows you're talking to him. The second word, the actual

command, should be accompanied by a tug on the leash.

One of two things will happen: the pup will come to you, or he won't come to you.

If he comes, consider it a miracle, but take advantage of that miracle. Pet him and praise him, and let him know he's done a wonderful thing. A tidbit is in order. Try him a few more times, then play with him and forget about the lesson until tomorrow.

If he doesn't trot right up to you, keep repeating the command and tugging on that leash. Don't pull him to you, but if he doesn't come, then do something else to attract him your way: slap your leg, snap your fingers, whistle, walk away, wave a tidbit, get down on hands and knees. It may take minutes, but he'll come. When he does, praise him and give him that tidbit. Try him a few more times and then call it quits.

Within a few days, the pup will be coming to you every time, or four out of five times. When that happens, close the doors—so that he can't run off—and try him off the leash. A couple of sessions should be sufficient, and then it's time to move him outdoors.

The chances are about even that he'll respond to the command outdoors. If he doesn't, then it's back to the leash method for a couple of sessions. The pup should respond every time to your command within two weeks.

If he doesn't, all it means is that he's a bit young for the task. But stay right with the command until he does respond, no matter how long it takes. "Come" is really the most important command of all, for it can save his life. When you see him dashing for a road someday, your call of "Happy—Come!" will turn him and bring him back to you, and the big truck's wheels won't be rolling over him.

Once the pup proves obedient to the command indoors and out, he's ready to learn heeling. And it's at this stage of his training that you'd be wise to invest in the right kind of training collar and leash. A metal-link slip collar is best—one that overlaps about two inches when pulled tight. The leash should be of pliable leather or fabric, and at least as long as you are tall, plus a foot or two.

Use this metal collar only when a training session is due. After a while, every time you put it on the pup, he'll know it means he's about to go to school.

And now, when he's ready for heeling, he's old enough to begin learning right from wrong. When he does something right, continue to praise him, but when he does something wrong, correct him. The correction should always be in words, such as "Bad dog!" Your tone of voice will mean more than a

whack. Physical punishment will only confuse him, and he'll resent both it and you. "Spare the rod and spoil the child" may work with humans, but not with canines.

"HAPPY——HEEL!" That's the proper command (with a pause between words), and when the pup obeys you he'll stay alongside your left leg, and his speed will be the same as yours.

The trick is to keep him even with you, no matter what your speed. Do this by holding the leash across your body, with the end and surplus in your right hand. With your left hand, tug on the leash and bring the puppy up to you when he lags, or back to you when he moves ahead. At first, the pup will probably try to charge ahead and pull you with him. If you can't bring him back with ease, reverse your direction, and he'll hurry to catch up with you. Keep repeating the "Happy—Heel!" whenever you correct him.

A five-minute session, twice daily, will have him heeling like a veteran in one week's time.

Now he's ready to stay at heel off leash, and your patience may be tested all over again. Be prepared, and have his leash in your pocket. When he doesn't heel free of the leash, deny him his liberty and give him a refresher course on the leash again. Sooner or later, he'll get the idea.

"HAPPY——SIT!"   It's back to the leash again when you teach the pup to sit. Place the student at heel position, so that he is standing close to your left leg.

·Hold the leash in your right hand. On the command "Happy (pause), Sit!" press down on the puppy's quarters with your left hand and yank up on the leash with your right hand. The yank shouldn't be severe. Make it just strong enough to lift his head. With his rear forced down and his front pulled up, the puppy is going to sit. What else?

Pet him and praise him immediately. Then repeat the performance, but don't prolong the session for more than a dozen tries. If he doesn't learn the command on the first day, he should on the second, and he most certainly will on the third.

When he does finally learn to sit on command, the time has come to combine his new talent with heeling. This training should also be done on leash. Again, hold the end of the leash in your right hand.

Ready? First, command the puppy to sit on your left. When he does, wait a few moments, and then give him the "Happy—Heel!" command. Step ahead, left foot first, and keep walking.

Ideally, the puppy will trot along at your side in heel position. But the first few times, he may be confused. If he is, he'll want to stay sitting.

In that case, remember the leash. It's in your right hand, and trailing across your left side. Grab the leash with your left hand and tug. The pup will come along.

If you've really taught him to heel, and really taught him to sit, the puppy will quickly put the two commands together in his mind and react in obedient fashion by the end of the first day's training session. And he may even anticipate the next thing you should teach him!

When you stop walking, he should stop, too, and sit. If he doesn't do that automatically on the first day, don't force him into it. Wait until tomorrow. Then if he doesn't sit when he's at heel and you come to a stop, order him to do so.

Once you have him sitting automatically, he's well on his way to being a well-trained dog, and you and he are a team. Three more commands—and each will be a breeze for him—and he'll really be well trained.

"HAPPY——DOWN!"   You want the pup to lie down, and it's one of the easiest commands to teach.

First, command the pup to sit. Then crouch before him, and as you give the new command, "Happy—

Down!" lift *gently* on his front legs. That will bring him down and give him the general idea of what the "Down" means.

Now go to the leash. Hold the end of it in your left hand. Stand facing the sitting student, leaving just enough room for the leash to loop about two inches above the ground.

Give the command "Happy—Down!" If he doesn't go down, step on the leash and pull it with your left hand. Don't be rough about it, and apply the pressure slowly.

If he still doesn't respond, try the foot method again as you push down on his back with your right hand. But only a stubborn pup requires that last step.

This is a good time to teach him the hand signal for the command. Once he's responding to the spoken word, or even while you're using the foot method, raise your right hand to shoulder level as if you're stopping traffic. It won't be long before all you have to do is call him, raise your hand, and he'll drop to the ground.

"HAPPY——STAND!"   Wanting your pup just to stand where he is may sound silly, but the command will come in handy when you're grooming him, or examining a cut, or don't want him to jump up and plant muddy paws on a visiting aunt or uncle.

The simplest method of teaching the pup to stand is to place him on top of a wooden table, box or crate. Make sure that the surface is firm and doesn't wobble. If he cringes at all, support him with one hand under the belly so that his TOP-LINE is even and his front legs come down straight.

Now keep repeating the command, "Happy—Stand!" and back off a few steps. You may have to keep correcting his posture, but nine times out of ten a pup will stand where he is rather than jump to the ground.

One or two off-the-ground sessions will be all he needs. Then repeat the lesson with the pup standing on the ground or floor. That's all. Tomorrow the pup will be ready for his final command.

"STAY!"   Note that the pup's name is not used with this command. The reason is a subtle one, but it makes sense: this is the one command that does not involve movement on the pup's part. By this time,

he'll be anticipating action of some kind each time he hears his name. When he gets accustomed to hearing the single word without his name in front of it, he'll stay right where he is—whether he's standing or sitting or stretched out on the ground.

It's back to the leash again when teaching this command. Preparation is the same as for heeling, so have the puppy sit on your left and hold the leash in your right hand. Now it's up to you to do three simple things at one time: (1) Give the command "Stay!" (2) step forward on your right foot, and (3) press back with the palm of your left hand against his nose. Next, turn quickly and face the pup.

The pup may move the first few times you try this, but you'll be just a step away, so push him back to the sitting position and try again. Sometime during the first session, he'll stay sitting as you face him. When he does, back off from him one step at a time, and keep repeating "Stay!" By the conclusion of the first session, you should be able to move the full length of the leash away from him.

On succeeding days, work him on the leash first, then remove the leash and walk greater and greater distances from him. And always, as you give the command to "Stay!" and step off, be sure to move your left palm toward his nose.

That movement of your left palm is another hand signal. After a while, the pup will recognize it as such, and then the spoken command won't be necessary. Every time you use that signal with your left hand, he'll stay right where he is at sit or stand or down.

If you stick with the short, daily training sessions, your pup will be fully trained by the time he's five or six months old, and perhaps sooner. There isn't any timetable for this. Pups—even pups from the same litter—mature in size and intelligence at their own rates, and there's nothing you can do about it. The runt can become the biggest dog in the litter, and the slow learner often ends up as a brilliant performer.

He'll look forward to his daily sessions and apply himself a little more, if you'll reward him with a good time. Try to find the time to play with him after each lesson, or take him for a walk or a swim. Whether he's been a brilliant student or a dunce, let him know that you're still the best of friends.

As your pet learns his commands, start using them away from the training sessions. If he begs when you're at the dinner table, have him sit at your side or lie on the rug. When you walk together, bring him into heel position part of the time. Your pup needs a little refresher course now and then, or he might forget what he's learned.

When your pup has the six basic commands down pat, it's time for you to congratulate yourself. You are now a proven trainer.

If your pup is a purebred, it's also time to consider the dog-show world. He's eligible for the shows when he's six months old, and the commands you've taught him are the ones he'll need to compete with you (as a team) in three dog-show activities.

Every year, more and more young people and their dogs are competing in these activities for prize ribbons, trophies (often cash), and fame.

Why not you and your dog?

IV

The Dog Shows

No matter where you live in the United States, there are dog shows in every season within convenient driving distance of your home. The shows are growing bigger all the time, and new ones are added to the list every year.

Despite their ever-increasing popularity, the shows do have their critics. Most of them consider dog shows to be no more than canine beauty contests, and that just isn't the case. The shows are held to determine the best dog of every breed present. A very few stop right there, but almost all continue to a selection of the best of the best dogs, or the one superior dog at the show.

Each breed has a written STANDARD of its own. Each standard is a precise description of a perfect specimen of the breed. The serious breeders strive to produce the perfect dog, and that's something like trying to find paradise on earth. Still, better dogs are being bred all the time and coming closer to the man-written standards, and that's what the phrase "improvement of the breed" is all about, and what dog shows are all about.

Over 900 licensed dog shows are held every year. "Licensed" means that they are staged (indoors or out, depending on the season) under the rules and regulations of the American Kennel Club. The shows are sponsored by local kennel clubs, and during the school year almost all of them are held on Saturdays and Sundays. And at almost all of them, three competitive activities are available for children and their dogs, so long as the dogs are purebreds, at least six months old, and registered with the A.K.C. All three call for a well-trained, healthy, spirited dog. And in all three, you and your pet purebred have a chance to win a measure of fame and some loot.

(1) *The Breed Ring*   This is the major activity, and the place where dogs win points toward the title of champion. There's a judge for each breed, a person who has proven to the A.K.C. that he (or she) is an authority on the breed, and it's his opinion—and only his opinion—that counts. It's up to the Beagle judge, for example, to decide which of the Beagles present are the best—or closest to the Beagle standard. Then he decides the very best of them all, or Best of Breed.

It's a matter of elimination. The judge runs through several classes of male dogs, and finds his blue-ribbon (first place) winner in each class:

Puppy: A dog under one year of age.

Novice: Any age, but has never won a blue ribbon in the next three classes.

Bred-by-Exhibitor: Any age, but owner-handler is breeder of dog, or member of breeder's family.

American-bred: Any age, but the dog was bred and whelped in this country.

Open: Any age, and the only class for dogs bred and whelped in other countries. Usually, experienced show dogs—some with CHAMPIONSHIP POINTS—are entered in this class.

From these blue-ribbon winners, the judge selects the best Beagle and names him Winners Dog. This one dog can win from one to five points, depending on the number of dogs he has just defeated.

Now the judge runs through the same five classes again, but this time he's selecting the best females. Just one becomes Winners Bitch, and she is awarded points, too, depending upon the number of bitches she has defeated.

To earn the title of champion, a dog or a bitch must accumulate 15 points. So the title can't be won at one show and takes a minimum of three. The minimum is seldom realized, for each show would have to be a 5 pointer, and that many points means a great number of breed members in competition. In any event, the grand total of 15 points must be won under at least three different judges, and two of the wins must be 3 or more points. This means that a champion dog or bitch must be a good one, for he or she has defeated many others of the breed at the 3-point shows. Winning 15 points at 15 shows, or a single point per show, wouldn't prove much, for the competition would have been limited.

So that's the point system, and points are won only by Winners Dog and Winners Bitch. Now things get a bit complicated. These two winners enter a class called Specials to compete for the title of Best of Breed against dogs who are champions of record. Here the competition is much stiffer, but one Beagle (either sex) will emerge as Best of Breed.

If Winners Dog or Winners Bitch is selected Best of Breed, he or she also wins the lesser title of Best of Winners. If neither is selected, then just the two of them compete for Best of Winners. While a lesser title, it's an important one in the point system, for one or the other may win more points.

Usually, more dogs than bitches are entered at the shows, so Winners Dog will earn more points than Winners Bitch. If he has picked up four points, they are his forever. But the lady may have earned only two points, for fewer of her sex were entered. Now, if Winners Bitch is selected as Best of Winners, she forgets her points and wins the equal of his. Both, then, win four points toward their respective championships.

All this doesn't mean that the weaker sex is favored. The reverse is also true, and on a day when there are fewer dogs than bitches present, Winners Dog can pick up extra points by defeating Winners Bitch.

It's the end of the day's activity for the one judged Best of Winners in this manner. Only the Beagle selected Best of Breed proceeds into another elimination contest known as Group. There are six such Groups, and the Beagle who is Best of Breed competes with the other bests of the other hound breeds in the Hound Group.

Before the show day ends, there are six Group winners, and those six compete for the title of Best in Show, meaning that this is the very best of the best canines of both sexes at the dog show.

The commands your dog must know for the breed ring are Stand, Stay and Heel. The judge must see the dog trot, and he must be able to examine the dog at close range. You and your obedient pup are ready for the judge.

(2) *Junior Showmanship*   You'll find other young people handling their dogs in the breed ring, but most of the handlers will be adults, and some of them will be professionals. While the judge is there to judge dogs and not handlers, the fact remains that experience counts, and sometimes a winning dog is not the best dog present. The professional handler, for example, knows just how to hide his dog's weaknesses and emphasize his virtues. There are fine points in every trade, and handling is the professional's trade. He earns his living by showing other people's dogs.

So handling experience is important, and there's a wonderful opportunity at the shows for you to gain that experience by entering the competition known as Junior Showmanship. This is a special activity for the young dog fanciers and their dogs. There's an age limit, and it varies from show to show. At some, it's open to boys and girls from the ages of eight to sixteen, and at others it's ten to sixteen. Again, the dog must be a purebred, and he must be owned by you or a member of your family.

The breed is unimportant in Junior Showmanship classes, for the competition is between the handlers and not the dogs. The action is the same as in the breed ring, but now the judge is keeping his eyes on the handlers and not the dogs. Once you've proven yourself a winner as a junior handler, you'll be more than ready for the breed ring and the experienced adults. You'll know just how to show your pup to his best advantage, and he'll feel right at home in the midst of all the noise and confusion at the dog show.

For the newcomer, Junior Showmanship starts with the Novice Class. You compete here with boys and girls who come within the show's age limits, and you remain in this class until you have won it. When that day comes, you are no longer eligible for Novice and graduate to one of the two Open classes:

Open A: For boys and girls up to the age of twelve.

Open B: For boys and girls from thirteen to sixteen years old.

No matter how much winning one does in the Open classes, the only way to move from A to B is become thirteen years old. But when you have won first place five times (in A or B or both) in a given year, you qualify to compete at the junior handling championship contest held each February during the WESTMINSTER KENNEL CLUB dog show in New York City.

Of the thousands of boys and girls competing in Junior Showmanship's Open classes, about thirty manage to qualify for a chance at this national title. So winning five times is not an easy task, and most of those who succeed manage to compete at about thirty or more shows every year. If you can't get out with your dog that much, don't be discouraged. There are trophies and prizes galore for first, second, third and fourth places in all three classes of Junior Show-manship, and the handling experience you gain will be worth even more.

(3) *Obedience Trials*   This is the fastest growing sport in the dog-show world, and trials are held under A.K.C. regulations at almost all licensed dog shows as well as separately. Whereas the breed ring is concerned with canine conformation, or comparing the dog to his standard, Obedience is a test of canine intelligence. Many a Best in Show dog is a failure in Obedience. Here the training you did with your pup will pay off, for the six basic commands are really the foundation work for Obedience.

In Obedience, you must handle your dog through a series of prescribed exercises, and his performance is scored by a judge. A perfect total score is 200, but a 170 score or better qualifies, and this is known as a leg. Three legs, each made under different judges, earns an Obedience degree from the A.K.C. Companion Dog (CD) is the first degree a dog can win, and then you can continue polishing his work and earn more degrees, each more difficult to achieve: Companion Dog Excellent (CDX), Utility Dog (UD), and Tracking Dog (TD).

Obedience competition is a true test of one's skill as a trainer and a handler. Your dog's success is really your own. And when he does well and achieves a high score, he's sure to win a valuable prize.

Since Obedience is a test of a dog's intelligence rather than a judgment of his breed qualities, the rules for dogs in this sport are not as strict as those for the breed ring. In both activities, the dogs must be purebreds, and they must be sound, but otherwise

Obedience rules are more flexible. A SPAYED bitch is eligible for Obedience, but she cannot be shown in the breed ring, for there she is not considered whole. Some breeds—such as Boxer, Doberman Pinscher, and Bouvier des Flandres—must wear a DOCKED tail and CROPPED ears in the breed ring (their standards call for this, although it can be argued that such dogs are not whole), but they can wear the tail and ears they were born with in Obedience. And then there's the big army of purebreds who are fine, healthy dogs in all respects, but they just don't come close to the breed standards and just couldn't win in the breed ring. They are too big or too small, too long or too short, or perhaps the coat color is wrong. So the dogs who wouldn't stand a chance in the breed ring can still be stars in Obedience.

There are some forty million dogs in this country, and most of them suffer boredom. They are expected to eat, sleep and behave. The majority are untrained. It's an easy life for the dogs. Too easy.

By nature, the dog craves some sort of action. So if nothing is planned for him, he'll find action on his own, and sooner or later he'll run into trouble. It can be simple trouble, such as tearing your best slippers into shreds. Or it can be a little more complex, such as turning over garbage cans, digging up your neighbor's garden, or chasing the policeman's cat. Or it can be fatal trouble, such as chasing one car and being killed by another.

But if you put his training to use, then the trained dog doesn't get bored and doesn't go looking for trouble. The training is work of a sort for him, and when he obeys your commands, he knows he's pleasing the boss. Of course, constant training without a goal in mind can become tiresome, too, for both the teacher and the student.

For hundreds of thousands of people, the dog-show world is the goal. And just by chance, the dog show has developed along lines that are ideal for young people. Fun, excitement and rewards are waiting for you and your purebred at the dog shows.

Entering the dog-show world is just as easy as

falling off a log. Every local kennel club that stages a licensed dog show once a year also stages several MATCH SHOWS. A match show is just the same as a licensed show, except that the results are not official. Thus, Winners Dog or Winners Bitch in the breed ring cannot earn championship points. In Obedience, a qualifying score does not count as a leg toward a degree. And in Junior Showmanship, a win does not qualify as one of the five needed for Westminster.

As far as the A.K.C. is concerned, all match-show wins are unofficial. Offhand then, a match show may sound like a rather silly affair, but it serves an important purpose. It is designed for newcomers, and is a dress rehearsal or practice run for the real thing. The match show is the place to give yourself and your pup some experience, and to find out if your dog has what it takes for the breed ring, and if he's ready for the Obedience trials. Some of the people you meet will be newcomers like yourself, and others will be veteran dog fanciers who are on hand to try out their own new pups.

At many of these match shows, purebred pups as young as three months old may be entered. Indoors and outdoors, over three thousand of these match shows are held every year, and some are closer to you than you may think. Finding out the dates and places of these match shows, and of the licensed shows, isn't difficult. Almost any breeder of purebred dogs will have the information, or somebody in the sports department of your local newspaper, or a veterinarian, or a member of the nearest kennel club, or anyone who shows his dogs or works his dogs in Obedience.

As things stand now—and they are not likely to

change—all this dog-world activity is for the pure-breds only. The organized activities for the mongrels are limited to two general areas: (1) The all-pet shows, which are usually held to promote something, such as the opening of a supermarket or a new playground; (2) Obedience training classes (not trials) held by private instructors, civic groups, 4-H Clubs, humane societies, and a few progressive kennel clubs.

So the owners of mongrels lack real goals. The dogs can't win championships or Obedience degrees. But the trained mongrel will always make a better pet. Few owners see it that way, which is unfortunate, but that's the way things are.

V

Exploding Myths

"It's cruel not to let a dog run loose"
For the dog's sake, he should run loose
only under supervision. Let's look at some startling
U.S.A. facts:

1) The stealing of dogs is a big, organized business. Despite new laws
to prevent it, over a million and a
half dogs are stolen every year.
Some are sold as pets in other
states, but most are sold to research laboratories.

2) A million dogs are poisoned every
year. Some of this poisoning is
intentional, for the nation is full
of dog haters. But much of the
poisoning is unintentional: a loose
dog may find and eat food meant
to destroy rats, or he may find and
eat a dead bird that was killed
through eating food sprayed by
deadly pesticides.

3) Three million dogs are killed by
automobiles every year. Even the
dog who is traffic-wise, and who
stands by the side of the road, waiting for a chance to cross, is not

safe. There are drivers who consider it great sport to deliberately
go out of their way and run over
a dog or a cat.

A wise owner will provide an escape-proof pen for
the dog who cannot always be supervised outdoors.
A 6 by 20 foot pen—with water, shade and shelter
—is big enough for any breed.

"Dogs must have bones for chewing"

This is a dangerous belief. Splintered bones may
choke a dog or pierce his organs, and they can break
his teeth. If you must tempt danger, then provide
a big, hard knucklebone. Better substitutes would be
one of the manufactured nylon bones, an old shoe,
or a knotted piece of leather thong.

"Dogs must eat meat"

They love to eat meat, just as you probably love to eat steak, but it is no more important to them than it is to you. Many kennels never feed meat. Food companies have spent millions of dollars in research to develop the best diets for dogs. Some of the dried foods have all the nutrients dogs require. This is the economical way to feed a dog, although he'll never object when you add meat or fish to his daily rations, as those additions always help to flavor the meals.

"Cats and dogs never get along together"

Nonsense. Still, it's wisest to start their association with ages in mind. A grown dog and a kitten, or a grown cat and a puppy. When both cat and dog are adults, the one who lived in the house first may resent the introduction of the other.

"The city is no place for a dog"

This is usually based on a lack-of-exercise premise. The truth is that the dog fits wherever man fits. The dog who doesn't run five miles a day doesn't miss running five miles a day. The same holds true for every man. And aren't we told by famous doctors that plain walking is the best of exercise?

"My dog has never had worms"

A dog without worms is a rare one indeed. From puppyhood on, almost all dogs carry one or more of four types of worms. No matter how healthy the dog seems to be, an annual checkup with the veterinarian—to determine proper medication—is an excellent idea. Today, worming is a simple matter.

Pups, of course, should be inoculated against the three dread diseases of DISTEMPER, HEPATITIS, and LEPTOSPIROSIS. Again, none of these shots are permanent, and annual BOOSTER SHOTS are desirable.

"Show dogs lead unhappy lives"

Show dogs are among the happiest canines alive, and they must be. If a dog is timid or unhappy, he is useless as a show dog, for he cannot perform at his best in the ring. And since he must get along on friendly terms with strangers and strange dogs, he makes a sociable, happy pet.

"You can't teach an old dog new tricks"

You can't convince anyone who says that of anything, so don't argue—just go right ahead and teach your old dog some new tricks.

"Teach a pup to swim by tossing him into deep water"

There is no better way to teach a dog fear of water. Always remember that the pup is a baby and treat him as one. If he won't enter water on his own accord, coax him in, or carry him in, but let him know that you're there to help him. Most pups, if trained first to retrieve an object on dry land, will then retrieve that object from water. But do it by easy stages: shallow water first.

"A dog makes a better pet than a bitch"

Half true. There are one thousand valid arguments in favor of the male sex, and another thousand in favor of the female sex.

"A cold nose means a healthy dog"

This is not a dependable barometer of canine health. Clear eyes, a nose that's neither dry nor running, pink gums, no excessive scratching, and a normal temperature (101.2 degrees) are better signs of good health.

If you keep regarding your pet as a human member of the family, common sense will guide the way you care for him. Treat minor scratches and cuts the way you would your own, for instance. But if your cut is deep, and you need a doctor, then your pet's serious cut needs the attention of a veterinarian.

Should your puppy act droopy, or you suspect there's anything wrong with him, check his temperature. If, over a period of hours, the reading remains more than one degree subnormal or above normal, rush him to the vet. You'll need a rectal thermometer, and keep the pup standing and quiet while you use it.

"A puppy with big paws will become a big
dog for his breed"

No more than a baby with big feet will become a giant. All of the puppy's parts seldom grow in balance. The pup with the biggest paws in the litter will probably achieve medium size, but he may not grow into the biggest member.

"Dogs live longer than cats"
Not so, but things are getting better all the time— thanks to research and advancements in medicine and nutrition. Life expectancies are currently rated this way: 14 years for dogs, 17 for cats, and 70 for humans. Those figures are for the United States, and the one for dogs should be considered as an average, since the life span for big breeds is usually less. Cats who reach 20 years are not unusual. Dogs are.

"Dogs need frequent baths"
Frequent brushing is fine, but soap and water remove the natural oils from the coat, so give your dog a bath as infrequently as possible. He'll keep himself pretty clean. When you must bathe him, keep soap and water away from his eyes and ears. Cleaning his ears with a damp cloth once a week is a good idea unless you have two dogs, then they usually clean each other's ears.

Too many people bathe their dogs, and too few pay any attention to their pet's nails. Most canine foot trouble is caused by long nails, and over half the dogs in America are never checked. Check monthly by standing the dog on a hard, even surface. Nails should be just short of surface. Trim back with special dog nail trimmer (available at most pet shops), clipping shy of end of vein. If you start when your pet is a pup, you'll never have trouble clipping his nails, and he'll never have trouble with spread feet or torn nails.

If your pup has DEWCLAWS, trim them back, too. Long ones can hook into something and rip back to the leg bone, causing the need for surgery.

"The dog's sense of hearing excels the cat's"

Dog and cat share equal senses of hearing and scent. In both departments, they are vastly superior to man.

"A puppy can have more than one father"
Wrong. Only one sire per pup. However, if the dam's owner isn't careful (as is sometimes the case with mongrels), each pup in a given litter can have a different father.

"If his food is moist, a dog doesn't need water"
Water constitutes over half the dog's body weight and is vital to all his body functions. He needs it just as much as he needs oxygen. If you cannot keep a supply of fresh water available to him at all times, at least offer it three or four times a day, and more often in hot weather.

Glossary

Adult	over twelve months.
Bitch	a female dog.
Booster shot	annual inoculation to continue dog's immunity to serious diseases.
Breed	purebred dogs, uniform in type and conformation, as developed by man through selective breeding.
Breed ring	judging area at dog show.
Canine	the dog family.
Championship points	points won by superior dogs in breed ring.
Clipping	trimming a dog's coat to achieve desired style.
Cropped	dog's ears cut so that they stand erect.
Dam	the female parent.
Dewclaw	a fifth toe (claw) found on the inside of the legs of some breeds; breeders usually have them removed in the pup's first week.
Distemper	most common of the infectious diseases, and biggest killer of dogs.
Docked	shortening of a dog's tail by cutting.
Dog	a male dog, but commonly used for both sexes.

Dog show	where purebreds are judged according to breed standards.
Domesticated	tamed by man.
Easy-keeper	not fussy about food.
Elbows-out	elbows not held close to the body.
Fear-biter	a dog who bites because he is afraid.
Grooming	brushing and combing to keep the dog's coat neat.
Hepatitis	a serious liver disease.
Hip dysplasia	a hip deformity that can occur in almost all breeds.
Junior Showmanship	a dog-show competition between young handlers.
Kennel	building for dogs, although some local laws say that a home for just one purebred dog is a kennel.
Leptospirosis	a serious kidney disease.
Litter	pups of one whelping.
Liver	color of deep, reddish brown, sometimes called chocolate.
Match show	informal dog show.
Mongrel	a dog of mixed-breed parentage.
Obedience trial	the proving ground for the well-trained purebred.
Otter tail	a thick, tapering tail.
Pack	a group of dogs, usually (today) hounds.
Pedigree	a three-generation record of any dog's ancestry; thus, both purebreds and mongrels have pedigrees.
Plucking	removing dead and broken hairs from dog's coat.
Puppy	dog under twelve months.
Purebred	a dog whose parents belong to the same breed.

Selective breeding	science of breeding based on the laws of inheritance.
Sire	the male parent.
Smooth	a very short, close-lying coat.
Sound	a dog without physical defects.
Spayed	a bitch who has undergone an operation to prevent her from breeding.
Standard	a written description of a breed's ideal dog.
Stern	tail of a hound or sporting dog.
Temperament	character as it affects conduct, as in humans.
Timber	bone, and usually heavy leg bone.
Top-line	even line along back from shoulders to quarters.
Variety	a division of a given breed.
Westminster Kennel Club	Westminster Kennel Club sponsors the world's oldest dog show (1877), and many consider it the world's most important dog show, too.
Whelped	a baby is born, a pup is whelped.
Wirehaired	a hard, crisp, wiry coat.
Withers	highest part of a dog's body behind neck, between shoulder blades, and used to determine height of dog when measured from ground.

Anatomy of the Dog

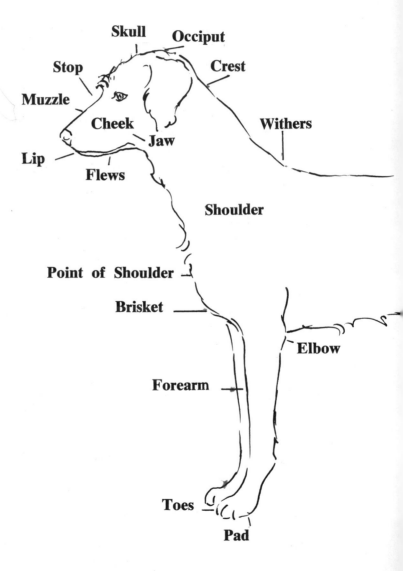

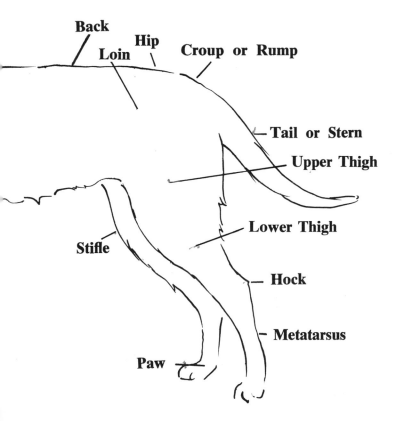

Back

Hip

Loin **Croup or Rump**

Tail or Stern

Upper Thigh

Lower Thigh

Stifle

Hock

Metatarsus

Paw

Index

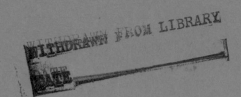